FLOWERS AND FRUITS
Stained Glass Pattern Book

Carol Krez

DOVER PUBLICATIONS, INC.
New York

Bibliographical Note

Flowers and Fruits Stained Glass Pattern Book is a new work, first published by Dover Publications, Inc., in 1994.

DOVER *Pictorial Archive* SERIES

This book belongs to the Dover Pictorial Archive Series. You may use the designs and illustrations for graphics and crafts applications, free and without special permission, provided that you include no more than four in the same publication or project. (For permission for additional use, please write to Dover Publications, Inc., 180 Varick Street, New York, N.Y. 10014.)

However, republication or reproduction of any illustration by any other graphic service whether it be in a book or in any other design resource is strictly prohibited.

Library of Congress Cataloging-in-Publication Data

Krez, Carol.
    Flowers and fruits stained glass pattern book / Carol Krez.
        p.   cm. — (Dover pictorial archive series)
    ISBN 0-486-27942-1
    1. Krez, Carol—Themes, motives. 2. Glass painting and staining—United
States—Design. 3. Flowers in art. 4. Fruit in art. I. Title. II. Series.
NK5398.K7A4   1994
745.4—dc20   93-46576
                                                                           CIP

Manufactured in the United States of America
Dover Publications, Inc., 31 East 2nd Street, Mineola, N.Y. 11501

PUBLISHER'S NOTE

These 60 practical and workable designs by stained glass artist Carol Krez feature a variety of flowers and fruits, all identified, chosen both for their linear grace and their variety of coloration as they occur in nature. The gorgeous and articulate rose designs will suggest opulent reds and greens to the craftsperson; in the supple shape of the plum the artist will envision rich purples. Other designs include camellias, rhododendrons, cherries and apples. The designs are sure to be either immediately helpful or inspirational for further personal projects.

Stylized iris, primrose, apple blossom

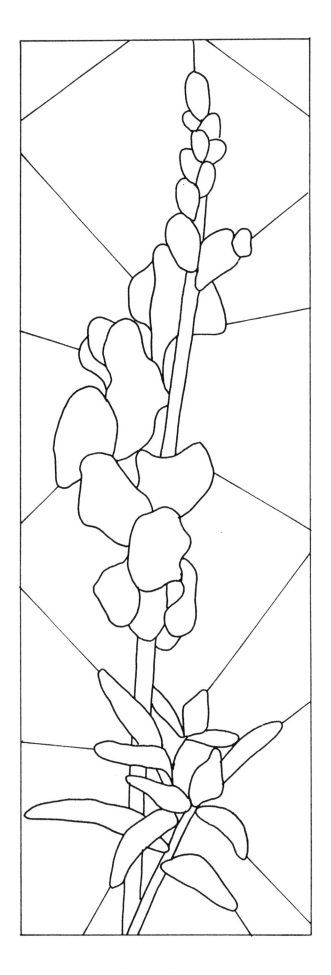

Snapdragon

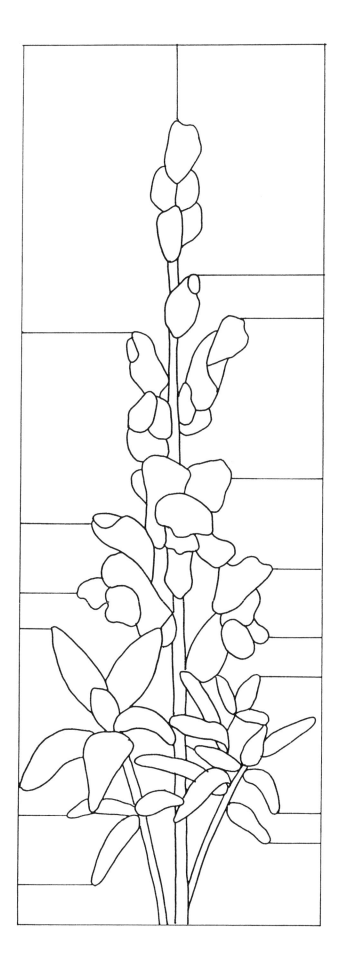

Snapdragon

Rose

Rose

Rose

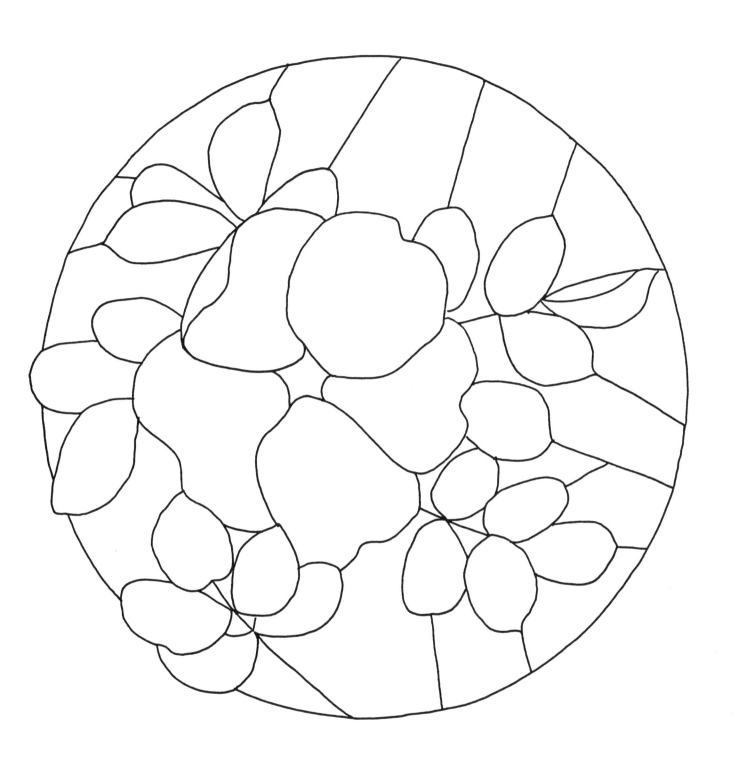

Salt spray rose

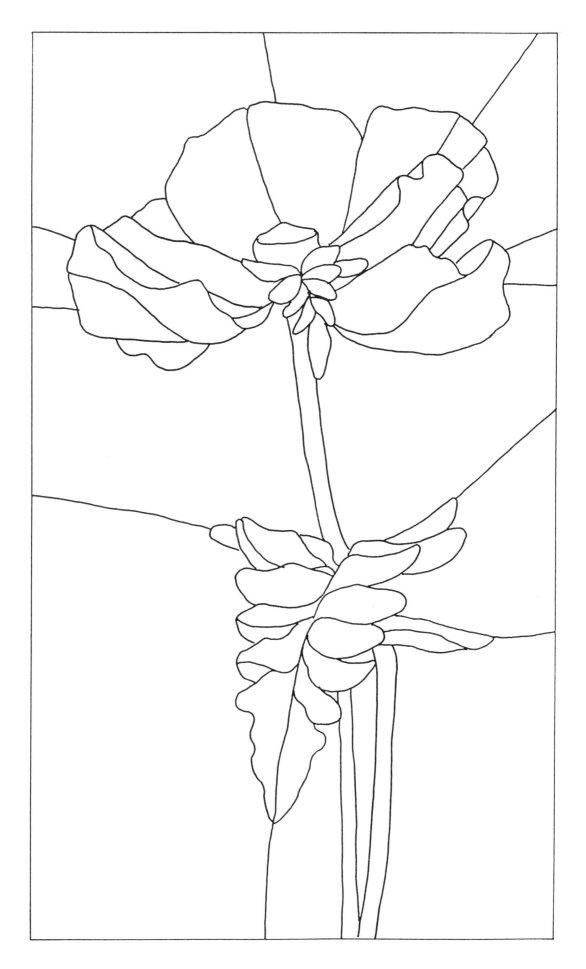

Oriental poppy

Oriental poppy

Oriental poppy

Oriental poppy

California poppies

Camellia

Camellia

Camellia

Flowering cherry

Flowering cherry

Flowering cherry

Cherries

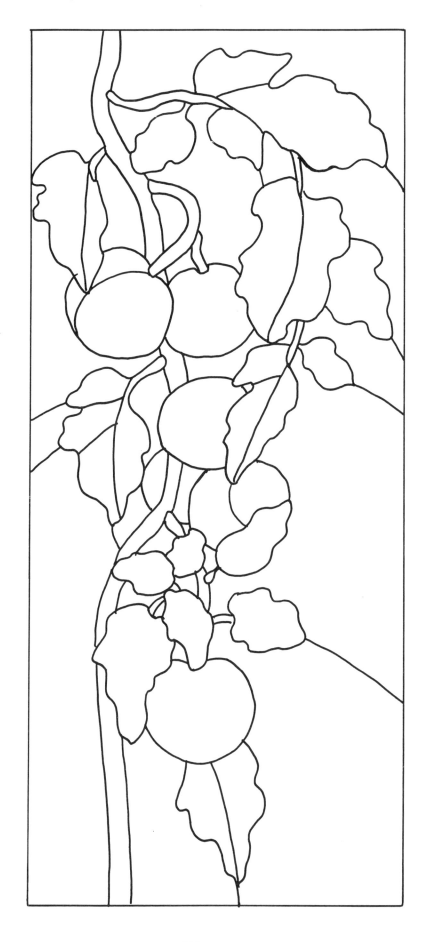

Tomato

Anemone

Anemone

Anemone

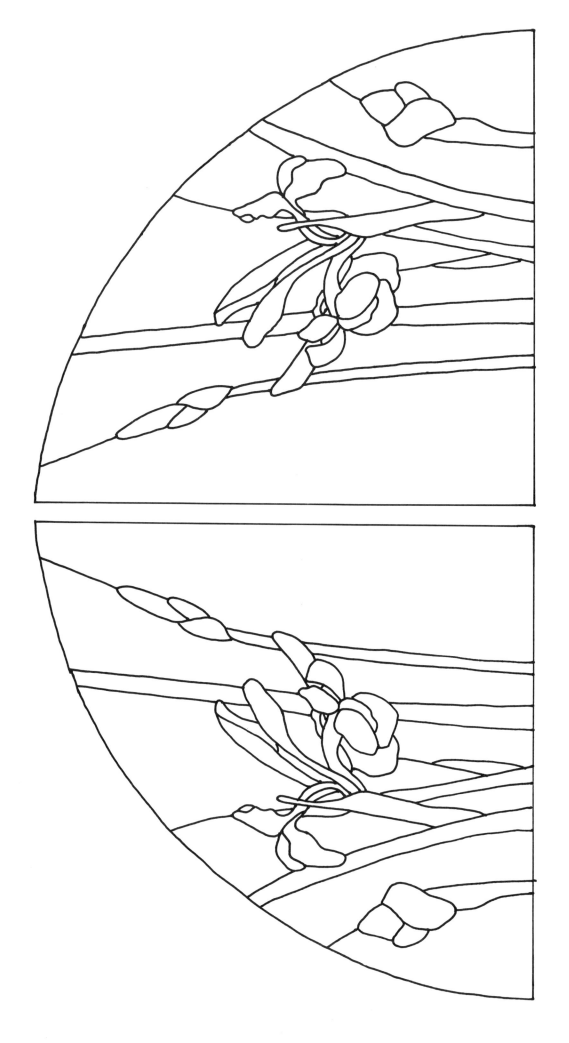

Iris

Iris

26

Magnolia

Geranium

Canterbury bell

Pansy

Oleander

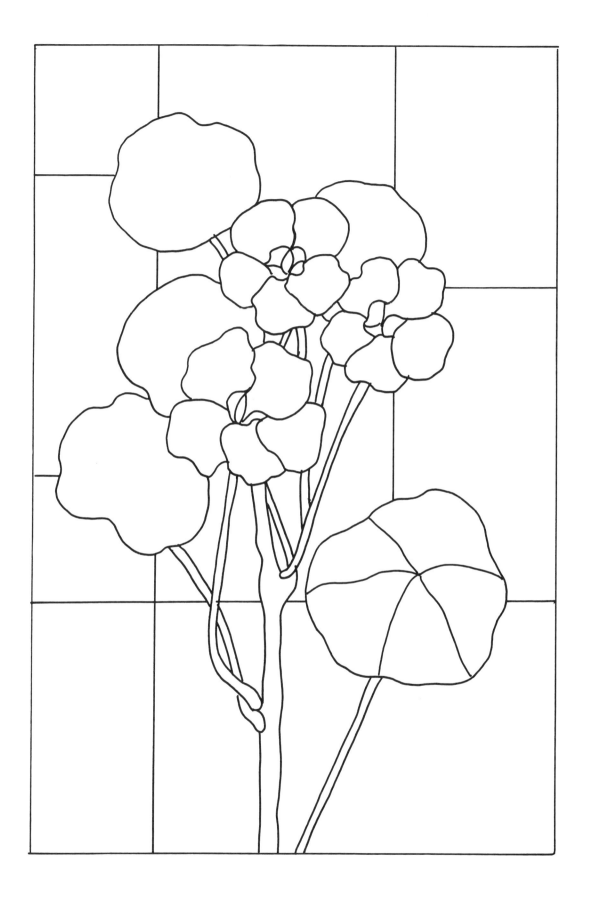

Nasturtium

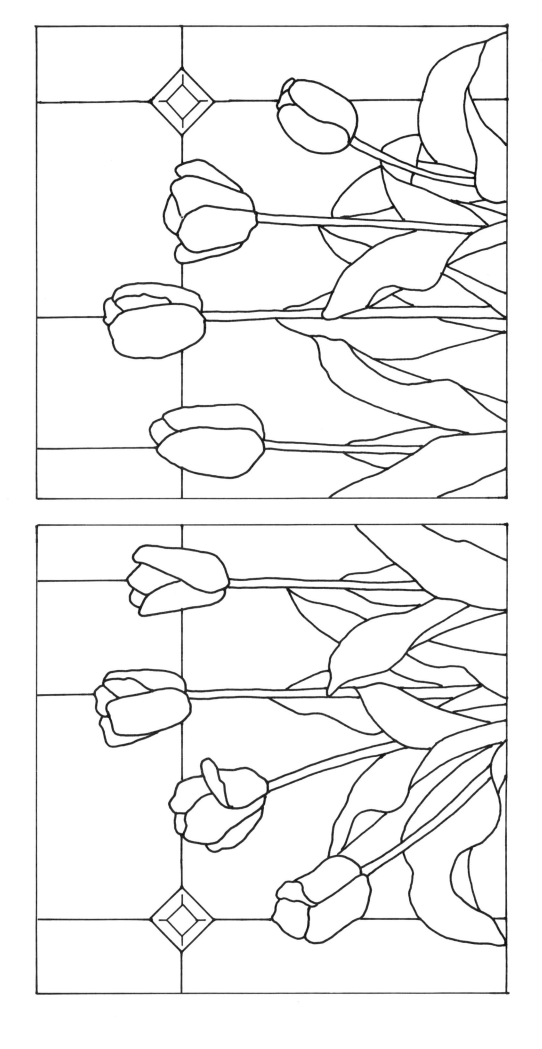

Tulip

Tulip

Apple blossom

Apples

Calla lily

Day lily

Day lily

Day lily

Lily

Peony

Peony

42

Rhododendron

Rhododendron

Rhododendron

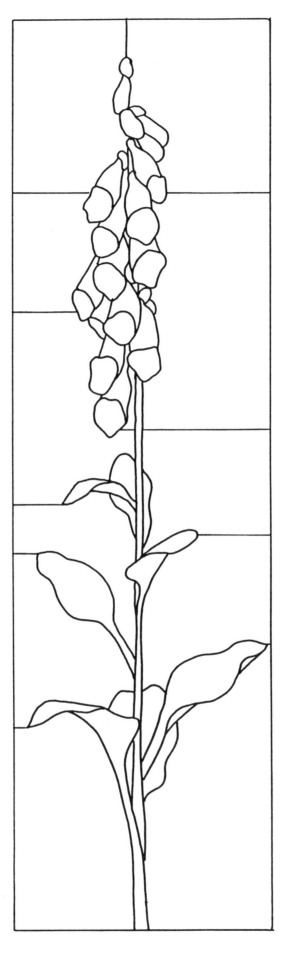

Foxglove

Foxglove

Figs

Daffodil

Plums

Plums

Crocosmia

Pears

54   Dahlia

Dahlia

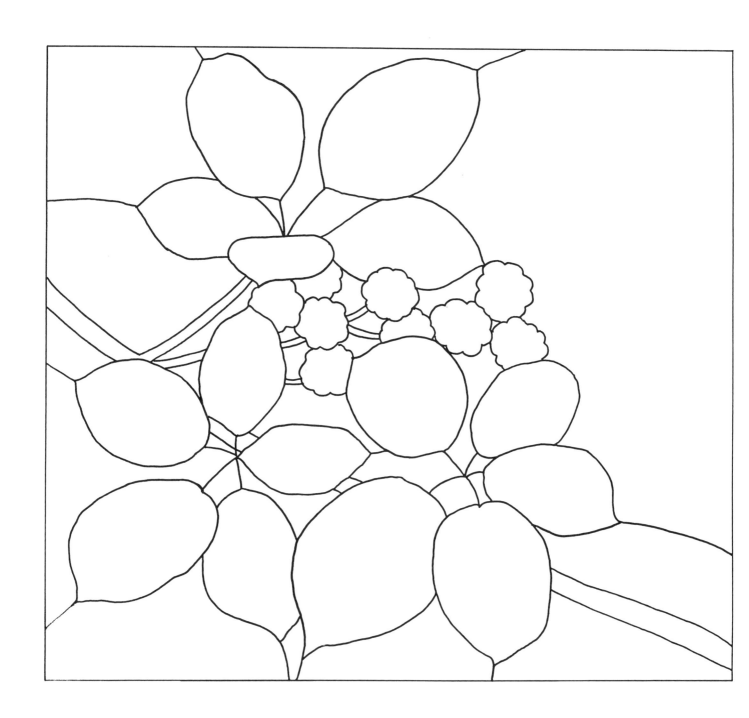

Blackberries

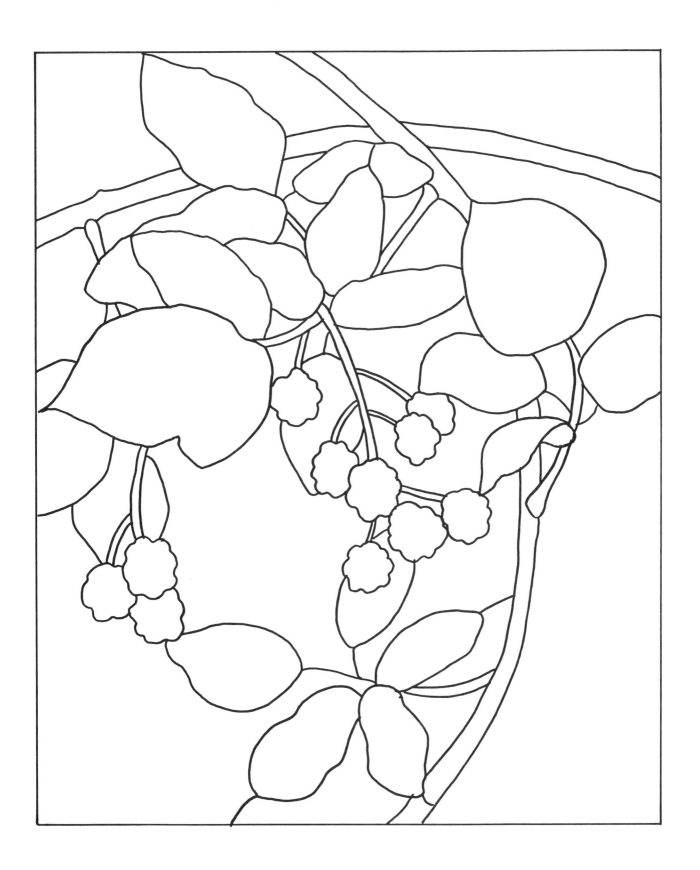

Blackberries

Gladiolus

Fuchsia

Hydrangea